HOW TO PURCHASE REAL ESTATE AT 0% INTEREST

To Help Sellers Get What They Want and To Accumulate Paid Off
Houses Faster For Your Retirement

ISBN: 978-0-692-97912-9

Interior Design: Christina Gorchos, 3CsBooks.com

TABLE OF CONTENTS

CHAPTER 1

HOW TO PURCHASE REAL ESTATE AT 0% INTEREST

While at the same time helping sellers get what they want and you also explode your net worth by accumulating paid off houses faster.

You may think that the title of this book, "How to Purchase Real Estate at 0% Interest", is impossible. If I had seen the title of this book about ten years ago, I probably would have not believed that buying Real Estate at 0% interest was possible. I would have thought this wouldn't work in my city or that I couldn't get it to work where I lived. I also might have thought that any person who would agree to a 0% interest loan wasn't making the right choice for themselves or they were being taken advantage of.

You may think that the title of this book, "How to Purchase Real Estate at 0% Interest", is impossible. If I had seen the title of this book about ten years ago, I probably would have not believed that buying real estate with a 0% interest rate was possible.

I would have thought this wouldn't work in my city or that I couldn't get it to work where I lived. I also might have thought that any person who would agree to a 0% interest rate loan wasn't making the right choice for themselves or they were being taken advantage of.

But all of these thoughts though couldn't be further from the truth. They are completely false and perhaps more importantly, they are limiting beliefs. False or Limiting Beliefs are erroneous, unconscious ideas that definitely limit what is possible for us when we choose to believe or indulge in them. Limiting beliefs show up in all areas of life and usually without us even being aware of them. Here are some common limiting beliefs that get in people's way.

"I'm too young"

"I'm too old"

"I don't have the time" or "I'm too busy"

"I don't have the money"

"I don't have the formal education"

"I don't care about _____"

I've noticed that there are at least three limiting beliefs that show up when it comes to and keeps people from buying real estate at a 0 percent interest rate. I will discuss these three limiting beliefs later in this chapter, but first I want to tell you why you should read this book and take action on the concepts shared here.

WHY YOU SHOULD READ AND ACT ON THE CONCEPTS IN THIS BOOK

I wrote this book because I didn't see anything else out there discussing this 0% percent interest rate buying strategy and it is so financially life changing that I had to share it. There are many Real Estate Investing books on the market. But, none were on specific on how to purchase Real Estate at a 0% interest rate and/or from someone who had done it several times. There are many books on purchasing Real Estate with nothing down. I've employed this strategy as well, however I've never seen one published about purchasing real estate at a 0% interest rate and how to do it. So for that reason, I had to share this strategy, so that someone reading this can know that it is possible and use it one day or many times in the future. I think purchasing at 0% interest can be as powerful or much more powerful than purchasing with no money down. Purchasing with no money down allows your return on investment to be infinite. This is true. However, with purchasing at a 0% interest rate, you create a situation for yourself to have a paid off property much quicker.

Through this strategy of suggesting to sellers to take principal only payments over time, I've been able to accumulate over $1,000,000 in 0 percent interest rate loans from sellers. I'm not saying this to brag but to instill belief in you that is possible for yourself as well. As a byproduct of this 0% interest rate, principal only payments strategy, I've been able to accumulate over $1,500,000 in very low interest fully amortizing loans at a 3-4% interest rate from sellers as well. Some sellers responded to my principal only payment 0% interest offers with an offer with interest. Some of those, I then accepted. Each of these seller financing based loans were made to me from sellers without a credit check, bank statements, tax returns, visiting a bank to get a loan, or speaking with a loan officer from a mortgage company. In the post 2008 world, getting a loan is a time consuming and somewhat of a painful process. For most all of my rentals, either getting seller financing or taking over the seller's loan, has been the only strategy that I used. Banks have so many rules as to the number of properties that you can have etc. that I don't like to deal with them. Between those 2 piles of 0% and 3-4% loans, that I was able to negotiate from sellers, my yearly principal paydown is now well over $150,000 per year. That means that every year, my net worth grows by over $150,000 tax free from this yearly principal paydown. This is all from focusing on this 0% interest strategy for 2 years. Yes, in just 2 years, I was able to accumulate over $2,500,000 in low interest loans from sellers.

My Story

Before beginning to invest in real estate aggressively, I worked as a Network Sales Engineer for 18 years. I skipped college, completed a 3 month computer technical school and went straight into the computer industry at the age of 18. At the time, taking on traditional college student loan debt seemed like not the best idea. Looking back, I'm grateful my parents didn't have the capital to fund a two or four degree because not having that as a default option helped to teach me resourcefulness. I entered the computer industry and because I was so hungry to be successful, moved up in the industry quickly. A couple of years after entering the industry, I became the youngest Systems Sales Engineer at Cisco Systems at the age of 21. Cisco Systems was one of the elite technology companies at the time like Apple is today. I thought I had made it. I was making over $140,000 a year as a 21 year old without a degree. I planned to stay at Cisco for 20 years and then retire. However, about a year after I was hired at Cisco in San Francisco, the dot com crash hit in late 2000, and then 9/11 happened in 2001, which caused even more tightening and layoffs in the industry. I made it through 7 rounds of layoffs, over the next 3 years, but in doing so my plan to retire with the company greatly changed as I was ready for something else. I was burnt out by the quarterly corporate stack ranking of myself versus my peers by different bosses, some of which that I had very little interaction with. I saw too many coworkers blindsided by the industry change and layoffs. I didn't want that to happen to me later in life, even though I made it through all of the layoffs. So at age 24, I made the commitment to be more in control of my destiny and to not be working for someone else by the time I had a family of my own. I spent my evenings and weekends intensively studying ways to get out of the industry.

After I left Cisco, I stayed in the industry for a while but I always felt a mental and emotional pain that I had to or was allowing myself to work for someone else. I wanted out of the rat race and grind of the corporate world. It always bothered me, that my destiny was controlled and limited by fear of going out on my own. I was also being controlled by the thoughts and opinions of administrators, bosses, or executives. I was always looking for a business on the side that I could have or build that would allow me to avoid the necessity of having to work for someone else. I explored many businesses that I could build or invest in that would help me make the transition from employee to being self employed and then from being self employed to being a business owner. Real Estate is what I used eventually to build a six figure income on the side prior to leaving working full time in the computer industry. It felt so liberating, when I collected my last paycheck. I knew then, if it was to be, it was truly going to be up to me.

It was such a fulfilling feeling to not have to have job to support myself and my family. I always felt somewhat controlled having an employer. I now run a Real Estate Buy, Fix, and Sell business in Northern California that buys 6-8 houses per month. I keep some of the houses that I buy as long term rentals using the strategies taught in this book. Through this book and my coaching course, Building Your Real Estate Buying Machine, http://www.realestatebuyingmachine.com I am actively helping many other people use the vehicle of real estate to get the financial freedom and financial abundance that they are looking for.

Let's talk now though now about some of those limiting beliefs that I mentioned earlier when it comes to buying real estate at a 0% interest rate. **Overcoming these limiting beliefs will definitely help you to close your first 0% interest deal.**

Limiting Belief #1

SELLERS WHO AGREE TO SELL AND CARRY-BACK A LOAN AT A 0% INTEREST RATE ARE UNSOPHISTICATED SELLERS

The sellers that have agreed to 0% interest with me have all been sharp enough to have paid off houses without inheriting them. In 2017, with over 50% of the U.S. population being just 1 month away from a financial crisis, that is a feat in of itself, to have a paid off property in the state of California where I have gotten all of my 0% interest rate deals. I know several people with graduate degrees that fall into the category of being 1 month away from a financial crisis and are considered by society, with their degrees and titles, to be very sophisticated and smart. All of the sellers that sold to me at 0% interest had net worth's of over $1,000,000 that they didn't inherit, but instead that they had created or earned for themselves slowly over time. One of the sellers that gave me a 0% loan worked as a loan officer for 25 years. Another seller was a landlord for over 30 years that had accumulated several paid off houses. Each of the sellers concluded that my 0% offers left them in a better monthly financial situation than they were in before our deal.

Each seller was actually improving their financial situation by selling to me at a discount and carrying back paper at 0%.

I would never do a real estate deal where the other party was not benefiting or did not know what they were doing. I strongly encourage you to operate the same way in all of your business dealings. Every seller should willingly sell to you and be happy that they are doing so. I still continue to have great ongoing relationships with every seller that has sold to me with 0% interest or at a discount. Later in this book I will be describing how every seller's situation has improved after selling to me at a 0% interest rate.

Limiting Belief #2
THIS WOULD NOT WORK IN MY CITY OR MARKET

This is a common limiting belief, but the truth is this strategy works any place where people have equity and in <u>any</u> market condition. Whether the overall market is rising, flat, or falling this 0% interest rate strategy works. At the time of this book writing, I purchased all my properties at 0% in a very competitive, low inventory California market during a time of 5-10% appreciation per year. Each of the sellers had many options to sell their properties. First, they could have chosen one of the thousands of realtors who were willing to list their properties for a traditional sale where the new buyer gets a new loan from a bank. They were aware that they could hire an agent to sell their house to a traditional buyer in 2-5 months. Second, all of my 0% deals have also been in big cities. Third, there are many other professional full time real estate investors in my market so there is plenty of competition. 0% interest deals are even appealing during declining or flat markets. However, those aren't the markets that I made my first $1,000,000 in real estate at 0% interest rate purchases in. I made them in one of the toughest of markets to buy in, so if I can buy real estate at 0% interest in an appreciating competitive market with low inventory, then you can surely negotiate a 0% interest deal in a flat, declining, or small to medium metropolitan area market.

Limiting Belief #3

BUYING AT 0% INTEREST ISN'T POSSIBLE AND THIS BOOK IS A SCAM

I've included in this book pictures of the actual promissory notes from my deals. Figures 1.1 through 1.3 on the following pages show the actual promissory notes for some of my 0% interest loans.

All of these promissory notes are notes from the seller to me. You can see that Figure 1.1 is for $190,000, Figure 1.2 is for $480,000 and Figure 1.3 is for $290,000. (Details on the properties and the seller have been omitted for privacy purposes) The promissory notes reproduced in Figures 1.1-1.3 are proof of the possibility of negotiating loans at 0% interest.

All of these properties break even, cash flow, or lose a little bit of money on a monthly basis. The loans range in time from 10 years to 20 years. **Each payment of $1520, $2000, and $2013 per month go 100% to reducing the principal balance of each loan each month.**

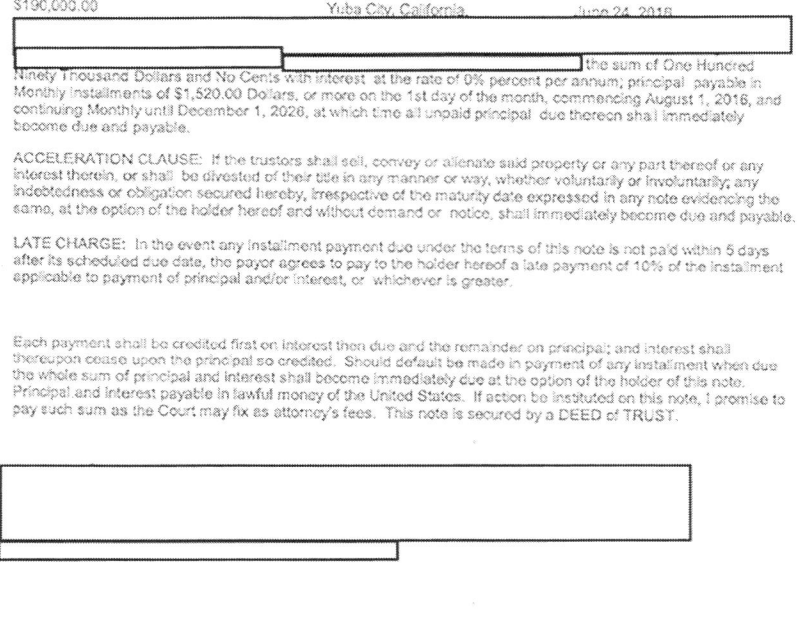

PROMISSORY NOTE
(INTEREST INCLUDED – DUE DATE)
(With Acceleration Clause)

$190,000.00   Yuba City, California,   June 24, 2016

the sum of One Hundred Ninety Thousand Dollars and No Cents with interest at the rate of 0% percent per annum; principal payable in Monthly installments of $1,520.00 Dollars, or more on the 1st day of the month, commencing August 1, 2016, and continuing Monthly until December 1, 2026, at which time all unpaid principal due thereon shall immediately become due and payable.

ACCELERATION CLAUSE: If the trustors shall sell, convey or alienate said property or any part thereof or any interest therein, or shall be divested of their title in any manner or way, whether voluntarily or involuntarily; any indebtedness or obligation secured hereby, irrespective of the maturity date expressed in any note evidencing the same, at the option of the holder hereof and without demand or notice, shall immediately become due and payable.

LATE CHARGE: In the event any installment payment due under the terms of this note is not paid within 5 days after its scheduled due date, the payor agrees to pay to the holder hereof a late payment of 10% of the installment applicable to payment of principal and/or interest, or whichever is greater.

Each payment shall be credited first on interest then due and the remainder on principal; and interest shall thereupon cease upon the principal so credited. Should default be made in payment of any installment when due the whole sum of principal and interest shall become immediately due at the option of the holder of this note. Principal and interest payable in lawful money of the United States. If action be instituted on this note, I promise to pay such sum as the Court may fix as attorney's fees. This note is secured by a DEED of TRUST.

DO NOT DESTROY THIS NOTE: When paid, this note, if secured by Deed of Trust, must be surrendered to Trustee for cancellation, before reconveyance will be made

Page 1 of 1 - 6/24/16

CA – Installment Note and Deed of Trust

Figure 1.1 Promissory note for $190,000 on a 0% Interest Loan

The promissory note from the seller to me in Figure 1.1 shows the terms of the note. The terms are for $190,000 paid in equal monthly installments until paid it is paid off. The time of payoff is in a little over 10 years with $1520.00 paid to the seller monthly with 100% going to the paydown the principal every month to pay down the loan. There are no interest payments.

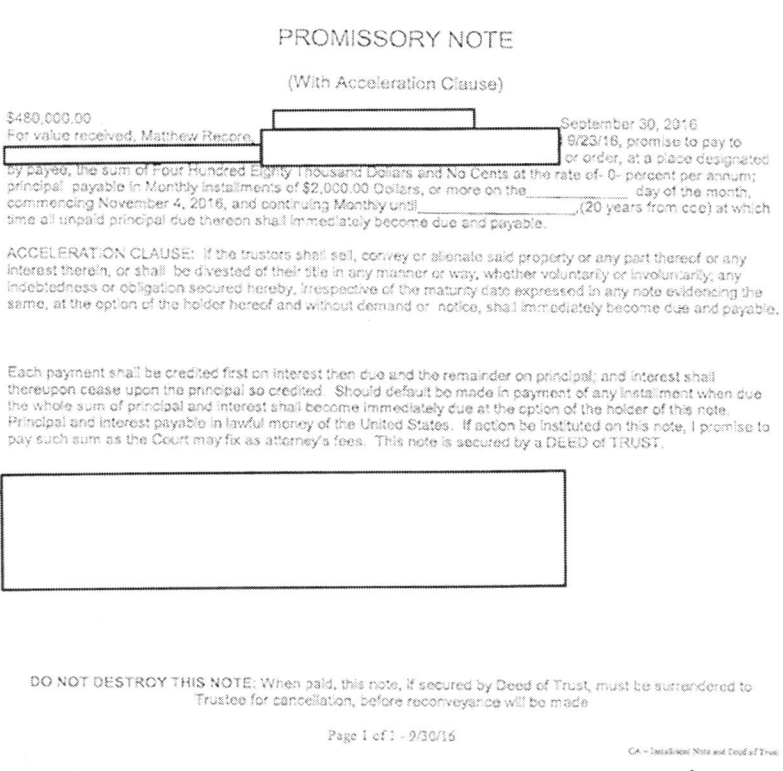

Figure 1.2 Promissory Note for a $480,000 loan at 0% Interest

Figure 1.2 details a transaction where I purchased a property for $490,000 that was worth about $550,000 at the time. I originally offered lower but the seller countered with a purchase price of $490,000, $10,000 down, and the $480,000 paid off over 240 months at $2,000 per month. $10,000 down equated to about 2% down and the seller carried back a loan at 0% interest for 20 years. This property is in a legitimate "A" neighborhood in a suburb of Sacramento.

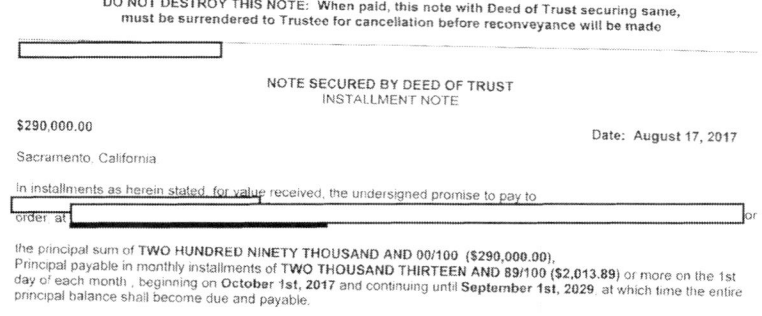

DO NOT DESTROY THIS NOTE: When paid, this note with Deed of Trust securing same, must be surrendered to Trustee for cancellation before reconveyance will be made

NOTE SECURED BY DEED OF TRUST
INSTALLMENT NOTE

$290,000.00

Date: August 17, 2017

Sacramento, California

In installments as herein stated, for value received, the undersigned promise to pay to

order at

the principal sum of TWO HUNDRED NINETY THOUSAND AND 00/100 ($290,000.00), Principal payable in monthly installments of TWO THOUSAND THIRTEEN AND 89/100 ($2,013.89) or more on the 1st day of each month , beginning on October 1st, 2017 and continuing until September 1st, 2029, at which time the entire principal balance shall become due and payable.

Figure 1.3 Promissory Note for a $290,000 at 0% Interest

This is from a house that I purchased for $300,000. I put $10,000 down (About 3%) and the seller carried back a loan at $290,000 over 12 years at 0% interest.

If I can do it, I'm confident that I can teach you to do it as well. Why do I say that? Because, I'm not that special. I worked as a Network Sales Engineer for about 18 years and prior to that I was a Network Administrator. I did work in Cutco knife sales in high school. But I don't have a heavy sales background and I don't have special negotiating or sales closes that I use to get our cash deals accepted or to get our 0% interest deals accepted. I think what I do is work hard. I also have a creative mind that gets to work on figuring out how to craft a solution to a seller's problems, predicament, or situation.

I mentioned earlier that prior to becoming a full time Real Estate Investor, I worked as a Network Sales Engineer for about 18 years. For about 14 of those years I didn't want to work as an Engineer anymore. I wanted to do something else. I wanted something, some business or source of income that would allow me to retire or quit the industry. As each year went by, I hated being an employee and working for someone else even more. I was too afraid to quit though.

This concept continued to exist in my mind-

An Entrepreneur is a person who risks their own money for freedom rather than exchanging their freedom for money.

Eventually I started investing in real estate on the side while I worked full time. As I refined my systems over several years, I built up a six figure income on the side flipping houses while keeping my full time job. That six figure income continued to grow until I could comfortably walk away from being an engineer.

While flipping houses using the systems that I developed and refined I was able to get more 0% and low interest seller finance deals. To date I've purchased about 150 properties to buy, fix and resell and about 20 properties at below market interest rates given to me by sellers that I have held as rentals. All were win win situations like the other 0% interest deals that I share later.

On this website, http://www.0percentinterestrealestate.com, I will be continually sharing 0% and low interest seller financing deals that my company purchases to inspire you on your journey. You can also go to Facebook and type in "0% Percent Interest Real Estate" to join our Facebook group and community. There we will be sharing stories of 0% and low interest seller financing deals. There also may be opportunities for you to partner with other investors on their 0% deals.

PRINCIPAL PAYDOWN

This book is really also about principal paydown. This book is not about cash flow. Cash flow has tremendous benefits but there are thousands of real Estate and investing books that discuss the benefits of cash flow. As a full time real estate investor, cash flow is what you need to eat. In the short term, principal paydown will not put food on the table. You need cash flow from rentals or flipping as a full time real estate investor to do that. I am a huge proponent of having cash flowing real estate. A few of my 0% rentals cash flow. A couple do not. But more importantly what all of my 0% loans have in common is massive and quick principal paydown. **Since all of each monthly payment goes to principal, this principal paydown leads to a net worth explosion. My recommendation is to combine a significant cash flow strategy with a significant 0% interest principal paydown strategy.** That way you have the best of both worlds. One significant cash flow strategy is buying, adding value, and then selling homes quickly to generate chunks of cash to then use to offset breakeven fast principal paydown payments.

FULLY AMORTIZING LOANS

This book is also about the power of fully amortizing loans. A fully amortizing loan is a loan that is extends for the entire period of the loan. Meaning, there isn't a period during the loan where the entire balance is due. A period where a portion or all of the mortgage balance is due, is called a balloon payment loan. I am not a fan of balloon payment loans. I do have a few but they are manageable and I could pay them off with cash that I have saved or with a hard money loan if needed. I took on each one because I was buying the property at a significant discount. Fully amortizing loans, as we will discuss later, give you the benefit of getting a paid off asset. They also allow you to benefit from the most amount of principal paydown that takes place in traditional loans at the end of the term more than at the beginning. As we'll show in later chapters, this increase in principal paydown that grows significantly later is not the case with a 0% loan, instead with a 0% interest loan the principal paydown is large and constant from the beginning going forward.

MINDSET

I have chosen to not include much on mindset in this book. I could have expanded this book by over 150 pages if I wrote or added concepts on mindset. Mindset is probably 98% of building wealth. Without the right mindset,a person won't implement the strategies that I share in this book or in other wealth building books. Without the right mindset, a person will sabotage themselves or get in their own way. There are many books that help with building a wealth possible oriented mindset. Rather than write about mindset, I've decided to stay focused on the topic of 0% Interest and refer you to four of my favorite wealth mindset based books and five of my favorite quotes that apply to purchasing at 0% Interest.

Four of my favorites are-

- *Think and Grow Rich*

- *As a Man Thinketh*

- *Secrets of a Millionaire Mind*

- *Rich Dad Poor Dad*

Here are some quotes that can give you some inspiration in your 0% interest journey that apply directly to you getting 0% deals.

1. "If you believe you can or you believe that you can't, you are right either way."- Henry Ford

2. "You miss 100% of the shots that you do not take" - Wayne Gretsky

3. "There's always a way if you are committed"- Anthony Robbins

4. "Nothing has any meaning, except for the meaning that I give it"- Anthony Robbins

5. "Life gives you what you ask of it"- Garrett J. White

Each of these quotes directly applies to being successful applying the concepts of this book.

The lesson of the quote "If you believe you can or you believe that you can't, you are right either way." is that there may be some of those limiting beliefs that pop up that negotiating a 0% interest loan isn't possible. If you choose to believe that it isn't possible for you to get a 0% interest real estate deal, then it surely will end up being true.

The lesson of the quote "You miss 100% of the shots that you do not take" applies to this book in that I have made a lot of 0% interest offers that have been rejected. But, if I wouldn't have started making them, I wouldn't now have over $1,000,000 in 0% interest loans. Begin taking shots.

The lesson of the quote "There's always a way if you are committed" is if you are committed you can find the way or make the way. If you are committed to building a 0% interest rental portfolio, you can make that happen. We get in our own way much more than anyone else gets in our way.

The lesson of the quote "Nothing has any meaning, except for the meaning that I give it" helps in so many areas of life. It is always great to remember, that you are the one in control of every meaning. It's not what happens to you but the meaning that make that matters. If you have suffering around anything in your life, there's an opportunity then to look at your meanings about those things to reduce or eliminate that suffering.

The lesson of the quote "Life gives you what you ask of it" as it applies to this book is, if you never ask for a 0% interest loan from a seller and structure it as a win/win business scenario, you definitely will never get one. **I have never heard of someone receiving a letter, e-mail, or call from a seller offering to sell them their property at a discount and for 0% interest. You must first ask for a 0% interest loan to be given one.** (This statement was true until my 6th 0% Interest deal where I offered the seller a carryback opportunity at 3.5% interest. He accepted that offer but then when we met he said he wanted to counter my 3.5% interest carryback with a price that was $10k higher but at a 0% interest rate to keep the numbers simple. I had never suggested a 0% offer to this seller. I said Yes to his counter. So you don't have to always ask first, if you talk with enough sellers some will propose a 0% Interest offer to you. **You must also structure it so that their situation is better than anything they have ever had with the property.** As we will discuss later, there are certain types of sellers that are better to ask than others to increase your likelihood of getting a "Yes" answer.

BOOK SUMMARY

In this book I specifically focus on how I've purchased many properties at 0% interest and how you can too. At the time of this book writing, the 0% interest loans that I have received from sellers total over $1,000,000. I have asked for many more than $1,000,000 worth of loans. But the amount of 0% interest loans made to me total over $1,000,000.

The goal of this book is to teach and show you

- How to buy Real Estate at 0% Interest

- How to propose your offer to allow you to get a deal at a higher price that still makes sense for you

- Why a seller would accept a 0% seller financing offer and be better off with your offer

- Stories of my 0% deals so you can see that it is possible for you as well

I will show you can buy a seller's property at a 0% interest rate by detailing the scenarios of how I did. I will outline how both the buyer and the seller benefit. The seller will often get the price that they want and you will get a paid off house in a shorter amount of time. We have a community and a blog built at 0percentinterestrealestate.com and a Facebook Group called 0% Interest Real Estate for you to subscribe to inspire you on your journey to your first 0% interest real estate deal. My goal is to help over 100 people get their first 0% Interest real estate deal. Why? Because,

I want more people to get paid off houses faster to have financial and job freedom.

If you need help taking action of any of the concepts in this book or would like to build a full time business from buying and selling (flipping) real estate then visit http://www.realestatebuyingmachine.com. My team and I will support you on how to implement the concepts in this book and more.

CHAPTER 2

HOW DID I DISCOVER HOW TO BUY HOUSES AT 0% INTEREST?

How did I discover buying houses at 0% interest? I first heard about the concept from a real estate seminar called "The Multi-Millionaire Maker" that was being hosted by Bruce Norris in 2006. The market was changing and I was very afraid. I had just sold all of my California Real Estate thanks to listening to the well thought out advice of Bruce. I even sold my primary residence thanks to Bruce's advice and I was now renting.

Bruce was interviewing an investor by the name of Mike Cantu at the "Multi-Millionaire Maker" seminar. Mike Cantu is a successful real estate investor in Southern California and he was one of the speakers at the event. Mike mentioned just briefly that he had purchased a house with 0% interest. It didn't fully register with me at the time what he had said. I certainly didn't think it was possible for me to do it at the time. I also didn't fully understand the power of that possibility at the time, not like I do now. I was so filled with fear about the market crashing that I didn't think it was a strategy that would be effective at the time. It was also so out of the league of what I thought of as possible for me **that I didn't do anything about it for over ten years. Ten years went by before I actually began to implement it.**

Ten years later, after giving hundreds of offers to sellers, I decided to add in an offer with 0% interest. Then, one day, I got a call back and to my surprise, the seller accepted it. He said he wanted to sell the house to me with the principal only payments offer that I gave him. This is also known as at **0% interest.**

Why did he choose to say yes?

Because, in short, the offer met his needs. In this case, his previous tenant was paying him $900 a month, and after paying their property taxes, he and his wife were netting about $600 a month. This tenant was a friend of a friend, and they didn't want to raise the rent or go through the process of evicting them. They sold to me with the tenant in place, and I was willing to pay the seller $1520 a month net to them for the next 10.5 years. To me, that payment was manageable because I noticed that the market rent was $1650 per month. The rent has since risen to $1,800 per month.

If this tenant didn't want to pay the $1650, I knew I would work with her to find another place. I figured within

3-4 months I would get the rent up to the $1650 and yes there would be a small negative every month after I paid for taxes and insurance, but that small negative was worth it because I was going to have a paid off house in a great neighborhood in just over 10 years!

After I did it. I thought "Yes!". It was possible to buy houses at 0% interest!!! So I charged forward and starting making more 0% interest offers.

STORIES OF MY 0% INTEREST DEALS

The next five sections summarize the details of five actual deals I made in which I purchased the property at 0% interest. I am sharing the story of each deal in the hopes that they are an effective teaching tool. I want you to see the situation that the seller and the property were in and how I was able to structure a 0% interest deal and how it made sense for the seller to say "Yes" to.

Here Is The Scenario Of My 1st 0% Interest Transaction

The seller called my office to sell his property that was in a growing city near a large University of California college town. Prices and rents were on the rise at the time partly because of the short supply of rentals available in the college town nearby. This college town also has regulations that discourage building so that has caused an overflow of residents moving to the subject property's city because it is cheaper overall. The seller had a tenant that was a family friend paying $900.00 a month. The seller had no mortgage and after taxes and insurance, was netting about $600.00 per month. The seller was retired and wanted to receive a monthly income check higher than their current rent. The seller did not want to evict or raise the rent on this family friend but they did not object to me doing so.

Our Agreement and Deal

I paid $250,000 when the house was worth about $320,000 in fully fixed up condition. They wanted $60,000 down. They were willing to receive the $190,000 at $1520 per month over the next 125 months (about 10.4 years)

Here is how the numbers worked out for me-

I paid $250,000

If I were to fix the house and sell it at the time the **After Repair Value was $320,000.**

The house needed $40,000 in repairs to get to that $320,000.

It needed $3,000 in work to get a higher paying tenant in place.

Income	Expenses
$1650 in future rent in 3 months	-$1520 future mortgage to the seller
	-$200 a month for maintenance and repairs
	-$284 a month for taxes
	$1650 monthly -$1520 principal paydown mortgage payment= $130 gain -$200-$284= $354.00 per month in losses
	$354 x 12 =$4,248 per year in losses
	$4,248 per year in losses X 10 years = $42,480 in losses over 10 years

$1650 Rent Future Rent vs. current rent of $900.00 per month

Minus $1520 0% interest principal only mortgage to the seller

Equals $130 in a monthly gain

Minus $200 a month in maintenance and expenses

Minus $284 a month in taxes

= $354 per month

$354.00 x 12= $4,248 per year in losses

$4,248 x 10 years= $42,480 purchase price

So after paying $42,480 over the next 10 years but I will have a house worth over $300,000 that will pay me $1650+ for the rest of my life.

As a side to this story, a little over one year later the rent was up to $1,800 with a new tenant. So this property is now close to breaking even and will be paid off in less than 10 years.

> Would you pay $42,480 for an asset worth $300,000?
>
> That is the equivalent of purchasing this property for about 15% of the current value but paying it over time.

That's the power of buying a house that barely loses money or breaks even every month at 0% interest or with a low interest rate that pays off quickly. I was both shocked and excited when the first seller accepted the first 0% offer. Then, a couple months later another seller accepted my 0% offer.

It's proven to me that 0% can many times meet the seller's' needs. It can be the best decision for them-maximizing their monthly income, minimizing the headache of owning rental property, and giving them a comfortable life in retirement. Not to mention the tax benefits of spreading out their capital gains tax over multiple years. More on that benefit later.

Here Is The Story Of My 2nd 0% Interest Transaction

A potential seller of a house called me about a high end home that he owned that was worth about $550,000. The house was paid off. These are the exact notes from my assistant who received his first call into my office:

"Tom has tenants that pay $1,800/mo in rent. They are month-to-month and have occupied the property for over 2 years. Tom is very knowledgeable about the local real estate market and made sure to point out that he was formerly a loan officer and had a Real Estate Agent license. He said that typical rent for his property is 2,200-2,400/mo and that he was thinking about raising the rent. The property is in original condition. All that he has done is have carpets replaced and granite counter on a wet bar. He owns the property free and clear. He said that seller financing would depend on terms. He didn't shoot down the idea but didn't sound too into it either. He also wouldn't give a walk away amount, just wanted us to provide an offer."

We then had several conversations and ended up agreeing to a deal that worked for both of us. We agreed to a purchase price of $490,000. $10,000 down and $480,000 paid off over 200 months at $2,000 per month.

This is a very nice house in an "A" neighborhood and in an "A" suburb in the Sacramento Area. Something to note as well. I didn't get my credit checked to get this loan or any other 0% interest loan even though my credit is really good. The deal was put together through rapport, trust, and me meeting his needs.

His monthly income was going to increase from $1,300 ($1800 in rent- $500 for taxes and insurance) to $2,000 per month. He also wasn't going to have to deal with tenants or repairs costs. This was a win for him. The breakdown below details how it was a win for me as well.

Income	Expenses
$2,400 in future rent	-$2,000 mortgage payment
	-$500 in taxes and insurance
	-$300 in repairs and maintenance over time
	$2,800-$2,400= $400 per month is losses
	$400x12=$4,800 in yearly losses
	$4,800 in yearly losses x 20= $96,000
	So in effect on this deal I paid $96,000 to purchase a $500,000+ house

How many houses can you purchase for $96,000 over time that are worth $500,000 now, that don't require your credit, to become very wealthy? 1, 2, 3 ....? (So long as you can afford the negative $4,800 per year)

How much would a person pay over time if they purchased the same house on a 30 year fixed mortgage at the going interest rate?

On a $480,000 loan do you know how much someone would pay on the standard 30 year loan over time. Any guesses?

Here is a breakdown below.

On a 30 year loan the monthly payment on $480,000 loan would be $2,361.31 per month. For the 1st payment, $1,700 would go to interest and $661.31 would go to principal. Every month the interest payments go down and the principal payments go up, until the loan is paid off.

The current rate on a 30 year loan is about 4.25%.

Summary			
Principal:	$480,000	Payment:	$2,361.31
Interest:	4.25%		
Start date:	May 2016	Total interest:	**$370,072.13**
End date:	Apr 2046	Total payments:	**$850,072.13**
Term length:	30y		

So on $480,000 loan a borrower would pay over $370,000 in interest payments over the life of the loan!!!

For a total amount of payments of $850,072.13. Compare this to buying with 0% interest and paying $480,000 for the same property over 30 years. **This is why buying with 0% interest is how to accumulate paid off houses much faster at a much lower overall price.**

Here Is The Story Of My 3rd 0% Interest Transaction

I talked with a seller who wanted to no longer own a property. She said she was looking for a "win win" deal. She was a very nice and sharp woman who was over 70 years old. She wanted to not have to deal with her tenants anymore. She had a complicated relationship with them that went back many years. When I met the tenants, I noticed that many repairs had not been made in a very long time. The seller was very open to "subject to" financing because she had done it in the past and it was a good experience for her. "Subject to" financing is where the buyer takes over the seller's existing mortgage.

This is different from "assuming" the seller's mortgage where you get approved through the seller's bank and take over the note. When you assume a mortgage, your credit report and the credit report can become merged. "Subject To" deals are done without the bank's explicit permission. Title goes into your name you make their monthly mortgage payments. The other investor that she worked with before was honest, paid her mortgage on time, and ultimately paid off her mortgage.

Our Agreement and Deal

We agreed on a purchase price of $170,000. The house fixed up at the time was worth about $240,000. On this deal, I put $10,000 down, I took over her mortgage of $124,000 and she carried back a second mortgage of $36,000 at $600.00 per month over 60 months at 0% interest.

Her 1st mortgage was a 20 year mortgage at 4.1% fixed and there was 15 years left on the mortgage. The principal paydown on the mortgage was $425.00 per month at the time that I took it over. With my 2nd mortgage of $600.00, my principal paydown would be $1,000 per month. My plan was to hold the property for 5 years and the mortgages would be paid down to about $100,000. After 5 years, the property would cash flow about $500.00 a month and the house would be paid off in 10 years. Or I could flip it in 1-2 years if I felt like the market is peaking.

The seller was able to get rid of her property and the hassle of her problem tenants. I was able to get into a house relatively inexpensively at a discount, a small monthly loss, while I paid it down to flip it later or hold for the long term. Most of my flips, I use private or hard money but by getting a house with an existing loan and a 0% interest loan I am able to have a small loss until I flip the property. This deal was a low cost and low risk way to speculate on appreciation since there was so much principal paydown as well.

Here Is The Story Of My 4th 0% Interest Transaction

My 4th 0% interest transaction was one that I stumbled upon after agreeing to terms with the seller to take over their mortgage. This property was in a vacation area known as South Lake Tahoe. The seller was behind on their payments by $13,000. The seller said they had a modified mortgage with their lender 3 years ago. They said their mortgage was for 2% interest for the next 2 years and then it would adjust. The foreclosure auction was scheduled for 2 weeks out. I told them I would pay them $6,000 at closing, $1,000 when they moved out and pay their back payments of $13,000 to take over their loan. We agreed on those terms. After bringing their loan current and taking title to the property, I was able to see what their full loan terms were. Before taking it over I knew their balance was about $250,000. I found out that their $250,000 loan was broken up into two loans. The 1st was for $190,000 at 2% and their 2nd mortgage with the same lender was for $60,000. The total payment on that 1st mortgage is $1,000 with taxes and insurance. The lender, with the mortgage modification agreement created with the seller had taken $60,000 and put it on hold for the life of the loan. This is called a forbearance. This was an agreement that was somewhat common during the foreclosure crisis when banks didn't want to take back more properties. So they took a portion of the balance and put it at the end of the loan and then took the rate on the 1st mortgage down to about 2%. The 2nd mortgage for $60,000 was at 0% interest and was due in full when the 1st was paid off in 30 years or when the house is sold.

I partnered with a friend on this property to keep this house as a vacation rental.

Here Is The Story Of My 5th 0% Interest Transaction

My 5th 0% interest transaction was my probably the most creative and longest from beginning to end so far. The seller really thought through all of their options, interviewed 4 of my previous seller financing references, and asked for lots of personal information about me. In the end it all worked out. I'm sharing each of these examples to help you see how 0% deals can be done and greatly help the seller, so you can construct them as well if you like.

The house was a 2/1 1100 sq. ft house in an area of Sacramento that was becoming more desirable because of its proximity to downtown, the hospital, and freeways etc. When I sent my offer, with a few offer options, she said she liked my higher priced offer at 0% interest the best. She had received 2 other higher cash offers than mine from other investors, but she really liked my 0% interest offer. No other investor had included a seller financing offer. No other investor also presented a 0% interest offer. After she showed interest in the 0% offer, we scheduled an appointment for me to see the inside of the house. While looking at Google Maps before the appointment, I noticed that it had a detached 3 car garage adjacent to the house. This was very unique for the neighborhood. Many houses in the neighborhood only had a detached one car garage. During the walk through I saw an opportunity to convert the 3 car garage into a 1 bedroom 1 bath separate residence. I needed to confirm with my contractor how much that would cost to create. In that area, a 1 bedroom would generate about $1,200 a month in rent. My contractor came back with a figure of $50,000 to convert the 3 car garage into a 1/1 650 sq. ft house with a separate electrical meter and address. I figured also that if I remodeled the main house, it could generate $1,600 a month. The landlord had a long term tenant that wasn't taking care of the place and she was getting $1100 per month. After paying her property taxes she was netting about $850 a month. Rents had gone up a lot since she rented the property and she had not raised the rent. After taxes and insurance, she was netting about $850 per month because she didn't have a mortgage on the place. The numbers that we eventually agreed on was $300,000 with $10,000 down and $2013.88 per month to her over 12 years or 144 months. **$2013.88 net to her a month was over 150% more than she was making from the property.** My plan though was to put $40,000 into the remodel and $50,000 into converting the 3 car garage into a legal 1/1 on a separate meter and as a separate address.

This would bring the value up to well over $500,000 and make the house cash flow while it is paid off in 12 years. I told the seller what my plan was. She thought it was a good idea. She didn't want to do it though. She just wanted to sell the house as-is and start collecting her $2013.88 per month. She would rather not pay capital gains taxes and collect the note income. She didn't want to invest the money that I was going to invest into the property. It was also a win for her because with the $2013.88 that she was going to be getting she was going to be able to delay her Social Security monthly payout for another few years and begin getting more money from Social Security when she began collecting it because of her being able to delay it. This was another Win Win 0% interest scenario. The seller's situation greatly improved by selling to me with a 0% interest loan.

Here Is The Story Of My 6th 0% Interest Transaction

My 6th 0% interest deal was one that I didn't intend to get. I made an offer to the seller at 3.5% interest for a second mortgage of $50,000. The purchase price was going to be $250,000 with $200,000 being put down or as a 1st mortgage through another lender since they owed $190,000. The balance of the $250,000, which was $50,000 was offered to be paid back at 3.5% over 10 years. The seller accepted the offer but wanted to meet in my office to sign the paperwork. I said Ok. When they got to my office, they said they wanted to keep it simple. Let's just increase the sales price $10,000 to $260,000 and I'll pay him $500 a month for 10 years or $60,000 with 0% interest. I said yes because the house was in a great area of Sacramento and the ARV was about $360,000 and he said it didn't need much work and had a great tenant already in place. So I accepted the seller's counter of 0%. The seller end up being right. After the inside inspection, the house was upgraded inside and the tenants wanted to stay. So in summary my 6th 0% Interest deal was for $60,000 over 10 years at $500 per month on an "A" neighborhood property. 0% interest deals are possible and in great neighborhoods on great properties in great condition. Go make some 0% interest offers!

SUMMARY OF MY 0% INTEREST BUYS

0% Interest House #1 in Woodland, CA

- After repair value of $320,000
- House needed $25,000 in work to sell for $320,000
- House needed $4,000 in work to rent for $1650.
- Tenant paying $900.00 per month
- Market rent was $1650 per month

  Our agreement and outcome-
  - $250,000 purchase price
  - $60,000 down
  - $190,000 paid off over 125 months at $1,520 per month. 100% of every payment going to reduce the principal balance.
  - I raised the rent to $1650 after owning it for 3 months

0% Interest House #2 in Folsom, CA

- After repair value of $550,000
- House needed $20,000 in work to sell for $550,000
- House needed $3,000 in work in deferred maintenance
- Tenant paying $1800 per month in rent
- Market rent of $2400 per month

Our agreement and outcome-

- $490,000 purchase
- $10,000 down
- $480,000 paid off over 240 months at $2,000 per month
- Raised the rent to $2,400 after 5 months of owning it

0% Interest House #3 in Sacramento, CA

- Landlord was not happy with the tenants
- The tenants were not happy with the landlord not fixing issues.
- The house needed $7,000 in work to rent and $25,000 in work to sell for the After Repair Value
- The tenant was paying $900.00 per month
- The market rent is about $1,400 per month

Our agreement and outcome-

- $170,000 Purchase Price

- $10,000 Down

- Taking over 1st loan of $124,000 at 4.1% interest with 16 years left at $840.00 per month with taxes and insurance included.

- 2nd mortgage at $36,000 at 0% interest paid off over 5 years (60 months) at $600.00 per month

- $265,000 After Repair Value

- I put a new bathroom in place for the tenants. I fixed some other issues that they had. I raised their rent to $1,300 per month.

- MY PLAN- In 5 years the 2nd mortgage will be paid off. The 1st mortgage will be paid down to below $100,000. So in 5 years I will owe less than $100,000 on a $250,000+ plus house.

0% Interest House #4 in South Lake Tahoe, CA

- Seller was in foreclosure. Foreclosure auction was in 2 weeks

- House needed work

- Payment after back payments were brought current was $1,000 per month

- $65,000 0% interest second mortgage from Wells Fargo that I assumed along with the $190,000 1st mortgage at 2%. $350 a month paid to principal every month.

Our agreement and outcome-

- We negotiated a purchase giving them $6,000 at closing.
- Total purchase amount was $275,000. $25,000 in repairs.
- After repair value was $325,000
- Rented out for $1,300 per month

0% Interest House #5 in Sacramento, CA

- Seller was looking to retire and wanted to sell their property in As-Is condition
- Seller had receive several other cash offers
- Tenant was a hoarder and had below market rent
- House was paid off

Our agreement and outcome-

- My cash offer was lower than other cash offer but our 0% interest offer intrigued her.
- We went back and forth on time periods to amortize the loan over.
- She wanted a shorter timeframe. We settled on a 0% Interest loan over 12 years.

- In order to make that work, I figured I would have to convert the 3 car garage into a 1/1 620 sq. ft house. This would make the short term loan cash flow!

- Cash flow in a big city in California over short term loan is rare, but possible at 0% interest.

0% Interest House #6 in Roseville, CA

- Seller was looking to get income from some of their equity

- House was in a A- neighborhood

- Seller said the property was in great condition

- Tenant was great and wanted to stay

Our agreement and outcome-

- Seller countered my 3.5% interest offer with a higher price but at 0% interest

- I said Yes

- I close and increased the rent. House will have a small negative cash flow on Day 1 but $500 a month in principal paydown

CHAPTER 3

WHAT IS SELLER FINANCING?

Seller financing is just what it sounds like: instead of the buyer getting a loan from a bank, the person selling the house lends the buyer the money for the purchase.

The big difference between a bank loan and a seller financing loan is that with a bank loan you have about 4-6 options available to you- a 15 year mortgage, a 30 year mortgage, a fixed, or a variable rate. You are either qualified or not by the bank. **However, with a seller financed loan, you have a blank sheet of paper. You and the seller can create whatever terms that you want, so long as both of you agree on them.**

My favorite site for calculating seller financing options is at Karl's Mortgage Calculator.

https://www.drcalculator.com/mortgage/

This is the site that my team and I use to come up with mortgage financing options for all of my deals. My team and I are in the calculator several times a day. For 0% interest loans though, you don't need a mortgage calculator, just a regular calculator will due. We'll be going over how to come up with 0% interest offers a little later in this book, but in summary it is just the loan balance divided by the years divided by 12 months in a year to get the monthly payment.

I've done now over 20 seller financing deals. They are so easy, that I may never do another bank loan again. With seller financing, all of the terms and approval are done by the seller and the buyer. The terms are agreed upon, put into a contract and then sent over to escrow and title to write up. It is a much more simple process than getting a loan through a bank and having an underwriter or Fannie Mae guidelines determine if you are suitable risk or your financial situation fits into their criteria.

You can get creative with many things to make the deal work. All things are negotiable including

- the length of the loan
- the interest rate
- the balance
- the down payment
- the amount of principal paid down over time
- the adjustment of the loan over time

- when the balance is due or if it is paid off in full over time (amortized)

What I most often do is submit multiple seller financing offers at different price points and then let the seller choose. Or we use my multiple offers as a beginning of the negotiation.

One key thing to remember is that you want the property to be able to afford the mortgage, taxes, and insurance. If the rent coming in from the property cannot cover the mortgage, taxes, and insurance then there could be problems for you financially in the future.

Here are some pro's for both buyer and sellers.

Pros for buyers:

- Faster and easier closing – no waiting for the bank loan officer, underwriter and legal department to process and approve your application. Whatever you agree to with the seller can be written up by your title officer and closing can happen quickly

- Cheaper closing – no bank fees, appraisal costs, or points on the loan. Many times the interest rates are better as well. Most of the loans that I have received from sellers were below 4.5% which is better than the non owner occupied rate given by many banks.

- Flexible down payment – no bank or government required minimums. Many of my down payments to sellers are less than 5%. Once again, it is whatever you and your seller come up with and that works for both of you.

- It's a good option for buyers who are not able to secure a mortgage. Now that I have over 10 rental properties, it is harder for me to obtain traditional financing. With seller financing, those loan criteria or rules don't exist. Everything is done on a property by property basis.

Pros for sellers:

- Can sell "as is" – potential to sell without making costly repairs that traditional lenders might require.

- Good investment – potential to earn better rates on the money you raised from selling your home than you would from investing that sum other ways.

- Deferring of capital gains taxes. Rather than paying capital gains taxes in the year following the sale in one lump sum, the seller can extend the capital gains tax bill over the life of the loan.

- Lump-sum option – the promissory note can be sold to an investor, providing the seller with a lump-sum payment right away. If they want to sell the loan prior to the loan paying off for cash and liquidity, you could also purchase it from them at a discount.

- Security on the note- If the buyer happens to not pay, the buyer can foreclose, keep the down payment, and get the house bank.

- Many times higher prices than a traditional cash as-is sale or a higher interest rate than the bank would pay for the money to sit there

There aren't many cons for the buyer using seller financing except for getting yourself into a bad loan. A bad loan is one that either has too high of payments for the house, your situation, or for your savings. The cons for the seller is if the buyer doesn't pay then they will have to foreclose to get the property back. That can take several months depending on the foreclosure laws of your state. In California, that process from beginning to end takes about 4 months.

CHAPTER 4

SIDE BENEFITS OF MAKING 0% INTEREST OFFERS

To start off there are several disadvantages of making 0% interest offers to sellers. For one you will be rejected a lot. You will be laughed at as well. You might even be cussed out. You have to find a way for that rejection and criticism to not bother you. It helps to only make 0% interest offers to sellers that you are talking to personally and not through an agent. Most agents don't know what seller financing is, or anything about creative real estate. So if a house is listed for sale on MLS, your chances are lower of negotiating a seller financed deal, but it's still possible.

I know that for some people cash works best. For some people a higher price with 0% interest works better. You have to know that the seller is benefiting from your offer. **Everyone of the sellers that took my 0% offers in the previous chapter, benefited more by taking my offer**

than by staying in their current situation. Their financial benefits were that their monthly income went up and their tax situation was improved from a traditional sale. **By avoiding 20% federal and 13% state capital gains taxes on the lump sum of their capital gain, they saved some up to $120,000 in taxes that would have been due the next year.** By selling with an installment sale, they cut that bill down to almost nothing the next year and spread that over time. But by deferring it into future years, they give themselves the opportunity to fall into lower tax brackets in future years, the tax laws to change in their favor, or for them to have more deductions in future years to offset the gains. They all also didn't have to deal with tenants anymore. They instead got payments from me direct deposited into their account.

There have been some other side benefits of me making 0% interest offers. By making 0% offers I was able to hear the seller's counter offers or hear what they really needed in terms of seller financing. My 0% seller financing offers have generated over $1,000,000 in 0% interest loans from sellers. When those pay off, those will be paid off houses. The $1,000,000 in loans is great but it doesn't tell the entire story. Those offers led to the counter offers with interest. On many of them, I said Yes to their counter offers. I have had sellers counter at 3%-4% fully amortized over 15 or 20 years. I gladly accepted those offers. So while I have over $1,000,000 in 0% loans I have well over $1,500,000 in 3-4% fully amortized mortgages on very nice homes that pay down a lot every month in principal. All $2,500,000 in 4% or lower mortgages, did not require me to show income, assets, or get my credit run. I also could move those mortgages to other properties if I wanted to, unlike a traditional mortgage.

The concept of moving mortgages from one property to another is called substitution of collateral. Most escrow officers know how to do a substitution of collateral. Essentially, before you sell a property that has a mortgage that you want to move, you move that mortgage onto another property that you own. (An escrow officer will complete all of the paperwork with the owner of the mortgage and yourself to facilitate this process) Then you sell the property that had the mortgage on it and take in the proceeds that would of normally paid off that mortgage. I have used this moving of mortgage strategy to cheaply finance an "A" neighborhood house.

For example, you get great seller financing terms on a "C" or "D" neighborhood house that you also buy at a discount. Instead of flipping this property right away and getting rid of the great financing, another strategy that I have use is to keep the property as rental until you acquire an "A" neighborhood property that you want to keep long term. Close on the "A" neighborhood financing with a 6-10% hard money rental loan. Move the great financing from "C" or "D" neighborhood house to the "A" neighborhood while telling the seller that you are "upgrading" their loan to a better property with more equity. Most often they agree to the move because their loan is now secured on a better house in a better neighborhood. Then fix and sell the "C" or "D" neighborhood house and take the proceeds that you received in the amount of what the loan used to be to pay off the 6-10% rental loan. This is how to get great seller financing over to great properties.

Side Benefit Examples
3% INTEREST OVER 15 YEARS

I had one seller who sold me a house at 0% interest call me back. He was thinking of selling his next house traditionally with an agent but I told him that I wanted to make him an offer on the house. He said he wanted to make a little bit of interest on this next one with me but would take a lower price. He suggested the 3% interest number. I wanted the loan over 20 years or more but he suggested over 15 years. He wanted a higher down payment on this one than the $10,000 before. We agreed on $25,000. I paid $375,000. The current value for the property was around $425,000. What I loved is the current value, the "A" neighborhood, that it was the smallest house in the community, and that I could raise the rents so that the negative cash flow was manageable while the mortgage paydown happened very quickly. The principal paydown begins in month one at $1542.00 per month. My mortgage is $2400 per month. I've already raised the rent to $2150 per month and plan to increase it to $2300 by next year. My negative cash flow will only be about $500 a month with a principal paydown of $1550 and growing. This house is a net worth exploder while helping me on my taxes yearly by offsetting some other income.

As a side note, I could also always sell the house on a wrap at a higher interest rate, if the negative cash flow becomes too much for me.

CHAPTER 5

KNOW YOUR END GAME

Commercial Retail, Multi-Family, Section 8, Single Family Homes

'm a big proponent of knowing what your endgame is in real estate. There are many possible endgames. Here are some possible end games. Section 8 houses, commercial real estate, single family homes, or self storage facilities. Here are some end games.

Section 8

Commercial

Single Family Homes

Self Storage

What does that mean, knowing your endgame? It means knowing where you want to be long term. Actually knowing what your endgame is in every situation and what your outcome will be, is extremely important. What is your desired outcome in real estate? Is your endgame to go from single family homes to multi-family homes or apartment complexes? Is it to go directly into commercial and retail, or is it to go directly into multi-family? Is it to build a big portfolio of Section 8 rentals in low income neighborhoods, Section 8 rentals in good neighborhoods, or single family home rentals in great neighborhoods? I know one person whose endgame is multiple one bedroom, one bath, homes to put Section 8 tenants into. His name is Ward Hannigan. That's his endgame. Do you have an endgame? If so, what is it?

Here's a further description of Ward's 1 bedroom 1 bathroom end game. Ward is an investor that I greatly respect out of Southern California.

Ward was looking for a SUSTAINABLE, monthly income for when he retired, and would be nearly bulletproof...no matter which way the economy or politics dipped and swayed.

What he wanted when he retired was freedom, and the guarantee that we'd have the money to enjoy it--not a ball and chain.

So, starting out with a bias against rental units (because of negative experiences managing apartment houses) he decided to see if there was any other kind of income property he could stomach. Since he wasn't committed to any particular type he checked out the pluses and minuses of warehouses, storage units, office buildings, self-service car washes, RV parks, nursing homes, etc. But none of that more specialized real estate made him feel like he was really in control. He didn't want to deal with extensive overhead, employees, or be at the mercy of renting out special-use buildings or space to choosy tenants.

The turning point in his quest occurred when he discovered that we had been looking at the problem backwards by focusing on the different types of rental properties to invest in, rather than on the specific type of tenant he wanted to deal with. If he could define their ideal tenant then it would be a lot easier to see what kind of property he'd need to buy, to rent out to them.

He discovered that what he wanted was a quiet, non-aggressive, non-demanding, STABLE, older person with a guaranteed income. He was surprised, for instance, to discover that the most volatile influences affecting tenant turnover are changes in either their family make-up or job situation.

It became clear that a retired pensioner was the epitome of their idealized tenant. No kids or teens tearing up the property, no changes in family size that would cause a move to some other larger or smaller place, and no layoffs or out-of-area promotions or other job-oriented complications to contend with.

A 65-year-old retiree treasures peace and quiet. They are most happy and comfortable occupying a one bedroom, detached house in a predominantly single-family house neighborhood. They don't need a big backyard to take care of and most don't require a garage, since they don't want to deal with the expense of a car that they no longer need.

Once he knew the type of tenant he wanted, and thus the kind of property they wanted to rent, he decided to buy one and try it. In the years since he has discovered that hardly any other landlord wants to buy a one-bedroom dingbat to rent out-- especially those without a backyard or a garage and located in a low-income neighborhood.

So over the years, with his foreclosure profits, they've been picking them up at bargain prices. He modernizes the kitchen and bathroom, and paint and replace carpet with longer lasting laminate flooring. On the outside they put in modern, dual-paned windows and spruce it up with vinyl siding or a new stucco color coat, newly painted trim, a cleaned up yard, a mended fence and a smooth working gate.

At one time he had sixteen true dingbats in our rental portfolio and then foolishly he said he sold a bunch when the real estate market was booming. Now he is working to get back to a total of twenty of these gems this time around.

One bedroom, stand-alone houses are the most trouble-free, dependable type of rental he has ever experienced. His retirees are never late with their small portion of the monthly rent--and it seems that the only way they ever move out is feet first. Because of his exceptionally low tenant turnover, (about 16.2 years on average) his maintenance expense is quite low too.

He favors low-income tenants who receive a steady, monthly rent subsidy from the city or county (via HUD's Section 8 Program). That way he gets about 90% of our rent via direct deposit from the government and the remaining 10% from the retiree. And most years the government allows us a rental increase that's pegged to the current cost-of-living index applicable to the area.

He gets very few maintenance calls nowadays too, since he don't provide refrigerators, garbage disposals, or dishwashers. In turn he install leak-free faucets (Moen), grab bars, laundry hookups, a whole house fan and security screen doors.

His foreclosure profits are a key component in our ongoing effort to have all of our little houses completely paid off before he actually starts his retirement lifestyle. That way, no matter what economic upheavals occur, he'll still be able to rent out our free and clear properties at a profit.

And whenever he wants to scale down he can either hire a reliable property management company or sell the houses one-by-one.

He plans to get top price whenever he sell since he'll find and qualify the buyers and carry back all the financing, secured by our carry-back 1st trust deeds. In fact, the mortgage cash flow he'll receive should amount to much more than the rental income he'll be giving up by selling.

He used to think that he had to buy his properties within an hour's drive from us so he could manage them ourselves.

But in our hyper-inflated area (San Diego) even 90 year old dingbats, in lousy shape, were way overpriced.

So he branched out and started buying them in Phoenix, and are also looking for them in Bakersfield and Sacramento too. What he discovered is distance is no problem with dingbats since they are so "management free". They handle their management chores just like they do close to home… by phone and email. Yes, on those rare occasions when he has a vacancy he drives or flies to meet our new pre-qualified tenant to do the rent-up (the walk-thru, the rental paperwork, security deposit, rent receipt and hand over the keys)."

CLARITY IS POWER

Ward has a very clear end game. It's very important to be very clear on what your endgame is and why that is your endgame. Sometimes you actually can combine some of these endgames together. For example you can have some some single family homes, with some 1 bedroom 1 bath Section 8's, and some multifamily. Knowing why you want each one, and knowing what your endgame is, is very important.

Actually catering your endgame plans to whatever your personality is, what your strengths are, and the kind of lifestyle that you want to live is also very important, I've met several landlords of homes in lower income neighborhoods. Some of these rentals are Section 8 and some are not. These owners have to work harder and stay more involved, especially if they manage all the homes themselves, than the owner of a 200-unit multifamily complex that has professional property managers in place to take care of the day to day issues.

These 2 types investors have very different temperaments. I've noticed the Section 8 landlord and the upscale home landlord think of their investments differently. I've noticed they speak of their investments differently. Owners see their investments in a more relaxed and positive light when their homes are in nicer areas with well qualified tenants. These are the homes you want if you want fewer headaches. Homes in lower income areas require a more aggressive hands on owner or property manager.

The endgame is very important. Your endgame for your emotional state is also very important. What do you want to think about? What do you want your focus to be on, now and in the future? How do you intend to build that plan to achieve your goals? Where you want to be long-term is very important to figure out and to focus on. My goal with this book is to help you build a plan that will pay off financially and provide a secure and confident future for you and your family.

MY PERSONAL ENDGAME- MANY PAID OFF HOUSES IN "A" NEIGHBORHOODS

Like I discussed in the previous chapter, we all should know what our endgame is in the real estate investing world. There are several different endgames that can work out in the long run. They provide different amounts of income, both in quality and quantity of that income as time goes on. My favorite endgame, and the endgame that I am playing towards, is having many paid off houses in "A" and "B" neighborhoods, with no houses in "C", "D" or "F" neighborhoods.

What is an "A" neighborhood? An "A" neighborhood is a neighborhood with a great public school district. It has a very high median income for the area, and it's a place where parents want their kids to go to school. In every major city there's really, probably, 5-25 great "A neighborhoods and suburbs. Those areas are where I want to own rentals.

Why? Why do I like "A" neighborhood rentals? What I've come to find is that the houses stay rented longer with less tenant turnover. There is some turnover from tenants going out to purchase a home, but when they do leave they usually leave the place in great condition because they want their deposit back. I've also noticed that the homes are very easy to rent. They rent quickly to high quality applicants with strong and reliable jobs.

I really prefer to rent to people with strong qualifications and job histories, because I live in a state (California) where landlord/tenant law is skewed in the tenants favor. In other words, a tenant friendly state. Living in a tenant friendly state, it's very important that I rent to tenants that will take care of the property, that are honest and trustworthy people, and that have good jobs making good money. That really has to be part of your framework or else I've seen houses get destroyed on the inside. I also want to own in a neighborhood that my wife feels comfortable in after dark in the case that one day she needed to meet someone there in the evening. Properties I like to keep are the ones that are in those great "A" neighborhoods that will rent quickly to really high quality applicants. The other thing I noticed about "A" neighborhood properties is they don't have to be fully renovated or fully fixed up in order to rent and remain rented.

Because they are in an "A" neighborhood you don't have to spend an incredible amount of money on rehabbing them. People will rent it because of the neighborhood. They aren't as concerned with the countertops not being granite or small imperfections in the property. This leads to a larger net income for you over time.

Why am I not a fan of purchasing and holding for the long-term properties in F and D neighborhoods? For one, It can be expensive to fix them every time a tenant moves out. I've noticed that it's harder to find qualified and quality tenants who will take care of those properties as well as they do in the "A" neighborhoods. Also, renting to a qualified tenant in a challenged or bad neighborhood is a challenge in itself. Renting to an unqualified or poorly qualified tenant is setting you, and your unqualified tenant, up for failure. If things do go poorly, good luck collecting on any judgment that you may get for unpaid rent or property damage. While it happens in all neighborhoods, having trouble with tenants being unable to pay their rent is more prevalent in lower income areas. Unfortunately, some people will always have a reason why they can't pay rent for the month.. You can really be drawn in emotionally if you are not careful. I've fallen into this trap myself. I, myself, have become what I've heard to referred to as a "rent stalker" in the past- dealing with tenants where it feels like I am constantly waiting, wishing and hoping that the tenant pays the rent so that I don't have to go through with an eviction. I find that the eviction rates are higher in the F and D neighborhoods than in the A neighborhoods. Property values are also lower overall in these neighborhoods. Not all properties are "keepers" in my opinion. Some properties will make you better money short and long term being rehabbed to bring their value up and then sold immediately. These are the properties that I like to fix and sell.

These are all reasons why neighborhood is important whether you are going for a 0% interest long term rental or a quick "flip" to create a chunk of income.

This book is about how to make money utilizing the 0%, principal payment only method, so that is what we will concentrate on here. However, If you are also interested in rehabbing and reselling homes for profit as well you should visit our site http://www.realestatebuyingmachine.com.

> ## <u>This is my end personal rental game —</u>
>
> Accumulate great rental houses in great "A" and "B" neighborhoods, at bargain prices, with great terms that break-even or bring in cash flow, with fully amortizing financing or balloons that I can handle and that are good prospects for long term appreciation.
>
> I will flip the "C", "D", and "F" neighborhood houses. I may hold some "C" neighborhood properties on great terms with the goal to 1031 exchange them into an "A" properties in the future.

Houses that look like this

Dig Your Teeth In And Hold On

There were 13 houses that I had at one point around the city of Dallas, Texas. They were all in "A" neighborhoods. They all had fully amortizing, low interest rate mortgages. Yet, I sold them. I sold when the negative cash flow was getting to be too much. I had an increase in my personal expenses at the same time and I was hit with several tenants moving out at the same time leaving high repair bills.

I became filled with fear. I was very stressed. I forgot why I bought them. I allowed my personal expenses to get too large.

I got into a little bit of a cash crisis and unfortunately rather than digging my teeth in and hanging on, coming up with other ways to generate income and avoid losses, I panicked and sold most of them. I had 13 homes and I sold 11 of them. What would those 11 homes, all in "A" neighborhood's, be worth if I had held onto them? Now, 11 years later, they would be $2 million greater in value and that's **not** including the mortgage paydown.

What are some of the lessons in that?

The lesson is: when you have an "A" neighborhood house with a fully amortizing 30 year, 15 year or another mortgage it's best to dig your teeth in and hang on. Hang on for the most part in most all situations. Digging your teeth and hanging on, paying off the house and having a paid off house in an "A" neighborhood will pay you a lot over time. The lesson is don't give up and do whatever you can to hold on to the "A" neighborhood houses.

"A" neighborhood houses tend to go up more in value over time. They tend to be taken care of by tenants and they're easier to rent. The goal is to find a way to keep them. First: Don't Panic. You have options. If you can't keep them for some reason and you feel you have to sell, Consider bringing in a partner on them rather than just selling them off. Or, sell some of your interest in the "A" neighborhood houses rather than selling them all.

———

There are many things to consider when liquefying assets. What to sell? What to keep and why? If you're in that situation or if you want to partner on any of the properties that you may have, send an email over to **zeropercentpartner@gmail.com**, and we'll take a look at your situation and see if we can buy a portion or all of your interest in that property to help you out.

GOAL AND INTENTION SETTING

It is very important to have clear goals as to what you want. I have mine in writing. Our brain has a magical way of moving towards what we define that we want and that we focus on. What we focus on we move towards. So it's really important to be clear about what you want to create. Some of my sample intentions when it comes to Real Estate are-

Some of my Real Estate Intentions

10 Paid Off Houses in "A" Neighborhoods

100 Single Family Homes owned in "A" or "B" neighborhoods with great financing terms that cash flow.

Plans to get there

Buy, Fix, and Sell homes in "A" "B" "C", "D", and "F" neighborhoods that I am not able to get great financing on and keep the "A", "B", and "C" neighborhood houses with great financing terms eventually consolidating to just "A" and "B" neighborhood rentals.

CHAPTER 6

WHAT CREATES WEALTH IN REAL ESTATE?

Appreciation, Amortization, Cash Flow, Instant Equity, Location, Timing And Depreciation

The seven things that create wealth in real estate are appreciation, amortization, cashflow, instant equity, location, timing, and depreciation. I want to go over each one of these, because each one of these will contribute to your wealth and your net worth going up over time through real estate.

The first wealth creator is **appreciation**. Appreciation varies depending on the local market and circumstances, population influx, jobs, the overall economy, interest rates, affordability, and several other factors. It's something that we can't bank on as real estate investors, but you can greatly benefit from. Certain areas are highly cyclical with lots of appreciation in their up cycles and other areas are more linear and flat in regards to their appreciation.

The second thing that I really love about real estate and that really helps to build wealth is **amortization** over time. This book is really a book about the power of amortization. What is amortization?

Amortization Schedule				
Period	Payment	Interest	Principle	Balance
0				$200,000.00
1	$1,297.20	$1,125.00	$172.20	$199,827.80
2	$1,297.20	$1,124.03	$173.16	$199,654.64
3	$1,297.20	$1,123.06	$174.14	$199,480.50
4	$1,297.20	$1,122.08	$175.12	$199,305.38
5	$1,297.20	$1,121.09	$176.10	$199,129.28
6	$1,297.20	$1,120.10	$177.09	$198,952.18

Amortization is essentially the paying down of the loan over time. If you have a tenant in place, and they're paying you rent, they're essentially paying down your loan for you. If you happen to have cash flow on top of it as well, all the better.

In a 0% interest mortgage you are paying your loan down fast and in equal chunks or installments over time. This not like a 30 year or 15 year mortgage where the mortgage payment starts small and increases over time.

Cash Flow.

Cash flow is really simple. Your revenue, minus expenses, equals your cash flow. The goal is to have cash flow on every property that you own. If you do have a negative, there must be a very good reason for it, and it must be manageable. A very good reason is NOT the hope for future appreciation. I've seen many people buy with negative cash flow with the hope of the appreciation being greater than the negative cash flow. This can really cause challenges in the future. The best reason to have negative cash flow is in a 0% interest mortgage where the principal is paying down fast and you will soon have a paid off house. I am okay with having a little bit of negative cash flow on a 0% interest home for the simple reason that every payment is going to principal and that house will be paid off quicker. A 0% interest mortgage is kind of like a built in huge savings account because of the equity you are building fast.

Instant Equity.

Every house that I purchase I really want it to have instant equity. That's one of the rules that I always follow. I'm always walking into between 5%, 20%, 30%, or sometimes even 40% in instant equity. There's an old saying that you make your money when you buy. Well, this is one of the ways that you do that. You make money when you buy by buying in with instant equity. I have a coaching program that teaches this concept very thoroughly. It's called Building Your Real Estate Buying Machine. Visit my website at:

http://www.realestatebuyingmachine.com to learn how to build a six figure plus income while working full time like I did.

Location.

The other thing that really creates wealth in real estate is the real estate's **location**. Where the property is located and what is located around it is extremely important in real estate. What's behind it? What's in front of it? What's to both sides, and what's on the streets over and around it? What's coming to the area, and what has the area been in the past? Is an area on it's way up? Or, it's way out? All these factors combine to make up what's very important in the location of real estate. The better the location, the better the appreciation potential for that real estate.

Timing.

Timing, I think, is one of the most important things in real estate. They say location, location, location, is the most important thing in real estate. Well, in certain economies, like in California, it's timing. Timing is more important than location in California. Here's an example:

Purchasing a house in California, Florida, or Arizona in 2005 would have gotten you a very different price compared to waiting four years later to 2009. Bruce Norris of http://www.thenorrisgroup.com is who I've learned the most from when it comes to real estate timing. I highly recommend everything he teaches.

Depreciation.

The last thing that's very important is **depreciation**. Depreciation is the tax write-off that you're able to get on the property. This tax right off is virtual. It's not cash out of your pocket every month or every year. It's a benefit that you get from the federal and state government for owning the investment of real estate. The standard depreciation schedule for real estate is 27 1/2 years. This depreciation every year really helps a lot on your taxes. I highly recommend that everyone maximize their depreciation every year and get the full tax benefit of owning real estate. Another helpful idea: once you depreciate the house fully, you can always 1031 Exchange that "A" property into another "A" property and then begin depreciating that property over another 27.5 years.

CHAPTER 7

WHY PURCHASE PROPERTIES AT 0% INTEREST?

My favorite reason to purchase real estate at 0% interest is the rapid paydown of the mortgage to bring the house to being paid off. In a normal amortization graph of a 30 year fixed rate mortgage the bulk of the principal isn't paid off until the last 15 years. In the first 15 years, the majority of payments goes toward paying interest. **When you purchase real estate at 0% though you get the benefits of the end of the mortgage period but not having to wait 15 years to get to that point.**

In a 0% interest loan, the amortization is in a straight line just like in Figure 5-1. This creates an explosion of net worth because the mortgage balance descends progressively from the beginning and consistently over time. This is the not the case like a traditional mortgage balance paydown as shown in Figure 5-2.

Figure 5-1

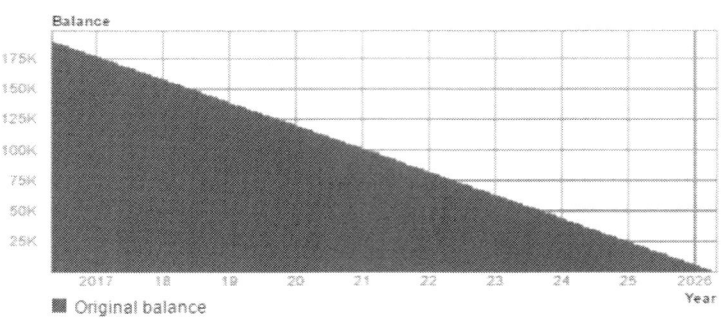

Figure 5-2

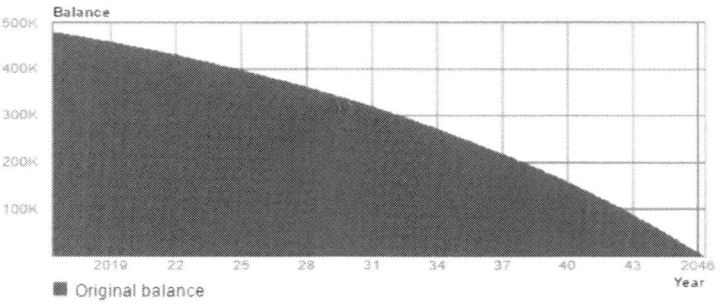

In a traditional mortgage, as you can see above, the first 10 years are rough in terms of mortgage paydown. The lender is getting rich off of you.A couple of years ago I surpassed the 10 year mark on a couple of loans and then I noticed something changed. My lender began marketing to me every month to refinance me into another 30 year mortgage. Every month I was receiving more and more marketing to get into another 30 year mortgage. This has gone on for over 2 years now. I wonder at what point will they give up that I'm not interested in getting out of my mortgage even at a little lower rate because the mortgage paydown is just now in my favor.

WHO WOULD A SELLER GIVE A 0% INTEREST LOAN AND WHY?

IDEAL SELLER FOR 0% SELLER FINANCING

After speaking with several sellers about seller financing and getting many to say "Yes" answers to it, I've come to find a several characteristics of that these sellers have in common. The <u>majority</u> of the sellers that have agreed to seller finance their properties to me at 0% and below market market interest rates have had their properties paid off. They all also were older than 45 years of age. They all wanted income more than they wanted cash. About 80% of them were interested in the capital gains tax deferral over time that they would be getting. And finally, They happened to all have had a motivation to not own or manage the property anymore.

Knowing the customer avatar of the type of seller that accepts 0% interest is really important. Can a seller who is 40 years old accept a 0% interest loan in a seller financed deal? Yes it is possible but I think it is highly unlikely. Actually I have never done a seller financing deal with a private seller (who also isn't a full time investor) who is less than 50 years old. All of the sellers that I have gotten seller financing from have been over 60 years old.

A seller is who is over 50 is more focused on the preservation of capital and income, rather than growth. So that is why carrying back a note with seller financing appeals to them. Prospects are great candidates for 0% interest seller financing. Suspects are those are don't make great candidates for seller financing. Below I've come up with a prospects versus suspects breakdown.

Prospects

Over 60 years old, house is paid off or with lots of equity, interested in monthly income, interested in deferring capital gains taxes, wants the highest sales price possible.

Suspects

Under 50 years old, little to no equity, interested in growth of the capital, not income.

SO, WHY WOULD IT BE A BENEFIT TO THE SELLER TO SELL AT 0% INTEREST?

There are several reasons why it benefits a seller to sell a property at 0 percent interest. One of those reasons is that you can offer a higher purchase price. You can also offer a higher income payment over time than they are currently getting from their tenants. They also will not have tenant hassles going forward. The final reason is they will have a lower overall capital gains tax by deferring that tax over multiple years rather than paying it in one lump sum the year after the sale. Higher purchase price, higher income for the seller, lower capital gains tax and no more tenant headaches- these are powerful motivators and are just some of the benefits that I highlight when I'm talking with a seller about principal only payments over time. Principal only payments enable seller financing on more expensive properties and enable it to be done in California. If I can do it in California, then I'm confident that you can do it in your state or in your city where, chances are, the prices are similar or higher.

What I've found from talking with my sellers who've accepted the 0 percent interest program is that each one of these were a huge benefit to them. Usually, one of them stuck out as being the biggest. For some, it was the purchase price near retail that they definitely wanted to get. For others, it was the higher income payments that made a lot more sense for them, or it was the fact that they weren't going to have to deal with the property or the tenants going forward; they were just going to get a reliable check or direct deposit from me every month.

The other day I was talking with a seller that accepted my 0% offer and he said "I don't need the lump sum cash. I'm on a fixed retirement income" "This offer eliminates me from having a huge capital gains tax bill next year. I also don't have to do anything with the property by selling to you."

DEFERRING CAPITAL GAINS TAX

The concept of paying for something on the installment plan is familiar to everybody. Instead of paying the entire cost of an item up front, you pay over the course of several months or several years. People commonly purchase items such as furniture or appliances on an installment plan. However, this method of payment is not limited to such household items. Consumers can purchase almost anything on an installment plan, including real estate. Installment sales of real estate have been around for many years.

INSTALLMENT SALES: ONE FORM OF SELLER FINANCING

Installment sales of real estate are a form of seller financing. Instead of borrowing money from a bank or other financial institution to pay the seller, the buyer borrows from the seller. The buyer and seller enter into an installment agreement in which the buyer agrees to make a down payment and pay the remainder of the sales price over a term of years. It can be one year or hundred, it's up to the buyer and seller to decide. The seller also agrees to pay interest on the payments. Again, it's up to the buyer and seller to agree on the interest rate—it can be higher or lower than the rates mortgage lenders charge. The seller ordinarily takes back a purchase money mortgage from the buyer. This way the buyer's promise to pay the seller is secured by the property—that is, if the buyer doesn't pay, the seller can foreclose and get the property back.

Tax Benefits of Installment Sales

Any sale in which at least one payment is not due until the following year qualifies as an installment sale for tax purposes. Such sales must be reported to the IRS using the installment method unless the seller opts out of using this method by filing an election with the IRS.

Under the installment method, the payments received by the seller are divided into two classes:

1. Gain from the sale, and return of the seller's basis (cost) in the property.

2. Taxes need not be paid on the portion of the payments representing return of basis--the amount the seller originally paid for the property. Tax must be paid on the portion representing the gain from the sale. This tax is paid at capital gains rates, which are usually lower than ordinary income tax rates. The seller must also pay regular income tax on the

interest paid each year. The following example shows how this works (for simplicity sake, the house sale price is $100,000).

Example: Liz sells her rental house to Rick for $100,000. Rick pays Liz a $10,000 down payment and agrees to pay the remainder in equal $10,000 installments over the next nine years, plus 5% interest. Liz paid $40,000 for the house and owns it free and clear; thus, her total gain is $100,000 - $40,000 = $60,000. This means that 60% of each payment represents gain from the sale, and the other 40% is return of Liz's basis. When Liz receives her annual $10,000 payments from Dick she'll have to pay capital gains tax on $6,000. She'll also have to pay tax at ordinary income rates on the $5,000 in interest she receives each year.

Why would a seller do this? Isn't it always better to get the entire sale price up front? Not always. There are many instances when getting paid over several years is better for a seller.

If Liz from the above example had been paid the $100,000 sale price up front, she would have had to pay tax on her entire $60,000 gain in the year of the sale. With the installment sale, she pays tax on $6,000 each year for 10 years. She pays tax on this amount at the 15% long-term capital gains rate, for a $900 annual tax. But she also is receiving interest payments from Dick on $100,000. This means that after she pays her tax she effectively has $99,100 earning interest. If Liz receives the entire $100,000 sales price up-front, she would have had to pay a $9,000 capital gains tax on her $60,000 gain the year of the sale. This leaves her with only $91,000 to earn interest.

COST SAVINGS OF INSTALLMENT SALES

Installment sales can also save sellers money if the income from the sale would put them in a higher tax bracket if they receive it all in one year. This is especially important for higher-income sellers who could be subject to the 3.8% net investment income tax that took effect in 2013. Single taxpayers with an adjusted gross income (AGI) over $200,000, and marrieds filing jointly who have an AGI over $250,000, are subject to this tax. Depending on their income, such taxpayers end up paying a 18.8% or 23.8% capital gains tax on their gains, instead of 15% or 20%. They key to avoiding this tax is to keep your AGI below these threshold levels. Using an installment sale can help you achieve this.

DOWN SIDES OF INSTALLMENT SALES OF REAL ESTATE

Installment sales are not for everybody. For example, if you own business property on which you've taken substantial depreciation deductions, an installment sale could be a tax disaster. This is because of depreciation recapture, which requires you to pay a 25% tax on the amount of the depreciation deductions you've taken. Even if you use an installment sale, you must pay this entire tax the year you sell the property. If you don't get a large downpayment, you may not have enough money to pay this tax.

If you're selling your home and qualify for the home sale exclusion, an installment sale may not save you any taxes. The exclusion exempts $250,000 of the profit from a home sale for singles, and $500,000 for married filing jointly. But, if you have substantial more equity than the applicable exclusion, an installment sale could be a good idea.

HOW TO FIND THIS 0% INTEREST SELLER?

There are several ways to find a seller who would interested in selling at 0% interest. Here are some of the ways that we get the deals in my office.

We find sellers on Craigslist, by using Google Adwords, bandit signs on the road, For Sale By Owner Websites, Direct Mail, Facebook Ads, For Rent signs that have individual owner managers, other agents, etc.

IMPUTED INTEREST

This is something that the seller will have to work with their CPA on after closing. If they sell at 0% interest the U.S. Federal Government will add an imputed interest rate to their return as income. Imputed interest is an estimated interest rate for a debt, rather than the rate contained within the debt agreement. Imputed interest is used when the rate associated with a debt varies markedly from the market rate.

When two parties enter into a business transaction that involves payment with a note, the default assumption is that the interest rate associated with the note will be close to the market rate of interest. However, there are times when no interest rate is stated, or when the stated rate departs significantly from the market rate.

Once the correct interest rate has been selected, it is used to amortize the difference between the imputed interest rate and the rate on the note over the life of the note, with the difference being charged to the interest expense account. So the seller will have to pay some taxes yearly on the difference between the 0% interest rate and the AFR (Applicable Federal Rate). Setting a rate with a seller at about 2.5% or above avoids this AFR tax.

CHAPTER 9

HOW TO PRESENT 0% INTEREST OFFERS?

There may be other ways to have get your 0% interest rate offers accepted by my preferred way of making offers is by written proposals. I think that an offer verbally carries with less meaning than a formal written offer that a seller can see in their hand to review. One of my philosophies is that every seller that calls our office, gets a written offer. That sets a really standard but I think a written offer shows that you are a serious. Which is what I am and I am a full time investor and I want to communicate that I am professional and serious.

The key goal in presenting a written offer and a verbal offer is to make them feel comfortable with you, to feel comfortable that you're going to be able to pay them every month no matter what. A seller that goes into a seller financing transaction with you does not want to foreclose. Sellers are selling you the property with seller financing and with 0% interest because they want to be paid. They want to know that they're not going to have to foreclose on you and they're going to get their payment every month reliably and on time. That's the confidence that I look to instill in my sellers and I want then to know that they will get those things by working with me.

As part of every proposal what I like to include is multiple offers. I like to present the seller with multiple options, not just a cash only option. There has been at least 3 times that my cash offer was too high compared to others, but my seller financing option was what they chose that was higher than the competitors cash offer. So this how I structure my offers.

Cash Offer- $100,000

Seller Financing 1- $110,000, $5,000 down, $105,000 mortgage paid off over 15 years at 4% interest at $776 per month

Seller Financing Offer 2- $140,000- $10,000 down, $130,000 paid off over 130 months at $1,000 per month

---

What to do?

Give multiple offers or options to each seller. Cash and 2 seller financing. One with interest and one with 0% interest.

What not to do?

Make 0% interest offers to houses listed on MLS in hot markets

---

CHAPTER 10

CHALLENGES THAT MAY COME UP

In the process of purchasing a few properties at 0% interest, I have come across a few challenges. Some of these challenges may be solvable on your own. Some may need a partner or a coach to help you through them. Some are not solvable. Getting resourceful is to how to solve most challenges. Here are the top four challenges that I have come across and some ways to solve them.

Challenge #1

THE SELLER ASKS FOR A LARGE DOWN PAYMENT

My goal always is to put as little down as possible when purchasing real estate. The only time that I have violated that rule is to get a 0% interest deal and to purchase my personal residence with my wife. Every other house for investment purposes has been with as little down as possible. My average down payment is $10,000. In one of the 0% interest purchases the seller asked for me to put $60,000 down. Fortunately, I had that amount in reserves so it worked out but in some cases you may not have those funds available. In those cases, I recommend that you partner with another investor or with a friend who has the money. If you happen to not have anyone in your life that is interested in partnering on your 0% interest deal, then e-mail me at zeropercentpartner@gmail.com. I will gladly either buy the contract from you prior to closing or we can partner 50/50. E-mail me and we will discuss it.

Challenge #2

THE SELLER REQUESTS A SHORTER AMORTIZATION TIMEFRAME OF LESS THAN 10 YEARS.

Your first offer to a seller as a suggestion may have an amortization period may be over 100 months, 150 months, 180 months, or 200 months. The seller may counter though with a very short amortization period of like over 5 years or 60 months. This very short amortization period of 60 months would most likely make the house negative cash flow. Meaning that the rent would be far less than payment to the seller. This might not make financial sense. If you split that negative 2 ways by bringing in a partner it might make better sense. Because each of you will have 1/2 of a paid off house in 5 years. So a negative every month might not be that bad if it meant having a paid off house in 5 years. If you come across this situation where the seller wants a short amortization timeframe, contact me at zeropercentpartner@gmail.com and maybe I can help you out and be that partner.

Challenge #3

SELLER COUNTERS WITH 2.5%-5% INTEREST FULLY AMORTIZING DEAL

This is a good scenario. If a seller counters your 0% offer at 2.5% to 4.5% interest over a fully amortizing loan then I would say that would be a great thing. A private 2.5%-4.5% interest fully amortizing loan is not as good as a 0% interest loan but it is still really good. Considering that with a seller carryback loan from a seller that you didn't have to get qualified and the loan doesn't show up on your credit, it is still is a great deal. I have several 2.5%-4.5% interest fully amortizing private mortgages that have been given to me by sellers. These are great. They are some of my best deals. Most of the properties cash flow, while the tenants pay down the mortgages.

Challenge #4

SELLER COUNTERS WITH A BALLOON PAYMENT DEAL

A seller may counter your 0% offer with an offer for you to purchase their property with a balloon payment involved. Balloon payments scare me. I've have four houses right now with balloon payments and they are one of the things that bring me uncertainty or anxiety about the future. With a balloon payment, when the balloon is due, if you don't have the money, then the seller can foreclose and take back the property. That is very scary. That is why I don't purchase properties on balloon's with more than $10,000 down because of the financial hit that you can take by not being able to payoff the loan when it comes due. So that is why I believe in being very careful with balloon mortgages and if a seller offers you one then you most likely want to pass unless you have the cash or can get the cash quickly to pay off the balloon mortgage when it comes due.

ENDING SUMMARY

Get sellers calling you. Listen to their needs. Start constructing 0% interest offers. Share the benefits of your offer. Follow up on those offers. If you still need some help after reading this book, would like a business that will get you 0% interest deals, then visit my consulting site at http://www.realestatebuyingmachine.com. We are currently buying about 6-8 houses per month. We will help you build a Real Estate Investing buying, selling, and wealth building machine.

Best wishes to you. Thank you.

Made in the USA
Lexington, KY
27 June 2018